Archangel Michael

Historical Roots, Symbolism and Cultural Impact

MARGARET BENSON

Copyright © 2024 - Margaret Benson

All rights reserved. This work or any part of it may not be reproduced or used in any way without the express written permission of the author or publisher.

First edition, 2024

CHAPTER 1. INTRODUCTION 5
Presentation of Archangel Michael 5
Purpose and Relevance of the Work 8
Analysis Methodology 12

CHAPTER 2. ORIGINS AND FIRST MENTIONS 16
Historical and Religious Context 16
Comparisons with Archetypes from Other Traditions 19
Michael as a Universal Archetype 22

CHAPTER 3. NARRATIVES AND LEGENDS 25
The Battle Against Evil 25
Other Narratives and Associated Stories 27
Cultural Variations in Legends 31

CHAPTER 4. SYMBOLISM AND ICONOGRAPHY. 36
Artistic Representations of Miguel 36
Symbol Meanings (Sword, Scales, Armor) 40
Miguel in Classical Art and Religious Heritage ... 45

CHAPTER 5. SPIRITUAL AND PHILOSOPHICAL ROLE 51
Michael as Protector and Divine Warrior 51
Ethical and Moral Implications 54
Psychology and Spirituality 58

CHAPTER 6. THE RELEVANCE OF MICHAEL OVER THE CENTURIES 63
Antiquity and Mythological Cultures 63
Middle Ages and the Ethics of Chivalry 67
Renaissance and Reformation 70

CHAPTER 7. MODERN AND CONTEMPORARY RE-READINGS **75**
   Modern Spirituality and Esotericism 75
   Popular Culture and Digital Media 78
   Global Syncretism and the Figure of Michael. 82

CHAPTER 8. ETHNOGRAPHIC RECEPTION AND CONTEMPORARY PRACTICES **87**
   Testimonials from Devotees 87
   Cultural Practices and Rituals 90
   The Figure of Miguel in Virtual Communities .. 94

CHAPTER 9. FINAL CONSIDERATIONS **99**
   The Universality of Michael 99
   The Future of Devotion to Michael 101
   Conclusions and Implications for Interdisciplinary Studies 104

BIBLIOGRAPHY **108**

CHAPTER 1. INTRODUCTION

Presentation of Archangel Michael

Archangel Michael occupies a central position in several religious traditions, standing out as a multifaceted symbol of protection, justice and spirituality. His figure transcends conventional descriptions of angels, assuming characteristics of a celestial warrior. As a defender of divine order and a fighter against chaos, Michael is a complex representation of protective forces, presenting himself as a model of courage and moral integrity. In the Judeo-Christian tradition, he is known as the "prince of the angels", leading the heavenly armies and serving as guardian of the righteous. In the Book of Daniel, he appears as the protector of Israel, while in the Apocalypse, his role expands, showing him as a leader in the final cosmic battle between good and evil. This character of Michael as universal defender of the righteous attributes to him a transcendent responsibility that inspires profound ethical and moral values.

In Islam, Michael is revered as Mikail, the archangel charged with distributing God's blessings and sustaining creation by maintaining cosmic balance. Rather than a warrior, Mikail assumes a more peaceful role, associated with mercy and ongoing protection. His function of preserving divine harmony highlights Michael's presence in a broader spiritual context, reflecting his role as a central figure of divine intercession. This interpretation reflects an expanded conception of the protector, where Michael or Mikail is one who upholds good, not necessarily with weapons, but by preserving cosmic balance and well-being.

Michael's symbolism is reinforced by the context of ancient mythologies, where he is mirrored in divine warrior figures such as Mithra in Persian tradition and Sekhmet in ancient Egypt. Mithra, for example, represents light and justice, and is invoked as a protector against the forces of darkness. Similarly, Sekhmet personifies protection, associated with war and healing, representing resistance to the evils that threaten order. The presence of these divine warriors in diverse cultures reinforces the archetype of Michael as a defender of truth and spiritual security, evidencing a universal human search for a protector figure. This need transcends cultures and eras, indicating that Michael is not simply a religious figure, but a reflection of human aspirations for an archetypal defender against evil and disorder.

On a visual and iconographic level, artistic representations of Michael are equally significant and powerful. Over the centuries, his image with sword, scales and armor not only illustrates his role as defender of good, but also communicates an ideal of moral authority and justice. The sword symbolizes the ability to discern and cut through falsehood, representing truth and courage; the scales are a symbol of divine justice and impartial judgment; and the armor reinforces the idea of spiritual protection, indicating the invincible strength of the virtue that Michael represents. The iconography associated with Michael has inspired and guided devotees in many cultures, reflecting a desire for security and righteousness. His presence in temples, churches and cathedrals is a visual manifestation of his spiritual authority and the collective trust placed in him as defender and guardian.

Michael's universality is reinforced by the fact that he is a figure of devotion across many traditions. He is not just an icon restricted to Christianity, Judaism, or Islam; Michael is an archetype that transcends religious and cultural barriers, expressing a deep human desire for a spiritual defender. His image as protector, judge, and warrior is an archetypal response to the needs for security and justice that permeate the human experience, whether in contexts of peace or adversity. This adaptability makes Michael a timeless symbol, capable of resonating across different eras and cultures, always representing the ideal of spiritual strength and moral integrity.

Finally, Michael is seen as an intercessor and protector, reflecting the human desire to rely on a strength that transcends human power. In times of adversity, he is invoked as one who not only protects, but also strengthens and guides, presenting himself as a source of hope and security for those seeking a path of righteousness. His figure personifies an ongoing struggle between good and evil, but also the certainty that, with protection and spiritual guidance, it is possible to maintain order and integrity in the midst of chaos.

Purpose and Relevance of the Work

The study of Archangel Michael offers a valuable lens through which to understand the deepest and most universal human needs, such as the search for protection, justice, and spiritual guidance. Michael is not just a religious figure; he embodies fundamental longings that span eras and cultures. Research on him allows us to explore how these desires have been expressed and reinterpreted over time, illuminating the persistence and transformation of core values for humanity. Michael appears as an archetypal protector, a defender of order and justice, who serves both to sustain the individual in times of crisis and to strengthen communities and traditions that seek to uphold high values in times of uncertainty.

This book aims to provide a comprehensive overview of Michael's origins and symbolic developments, mapping his cultural and spiritual impact from his earliest mentions in religious texts to his current manifestations in popular culture and contemporary spiritual movements. The interdisciplinary approach seeks to unite perspectives from history, theology, philosophy, and anthropology to embrace the complexity of Michael's figure. This methodological plurality is essential to unveil the many aspects that Michael represents: he is a warrior, a protector, a judge, and a figure of compassion. Each of these facets is revealed in different contexts, and together they paint a more complete and profound picture of how he resonates in the collective imagination.

Interdisciplinarity also allows us to capture the way in which Michael's image is shaped by historical and social changes, revealing him as a symbol that transcends any singular interpretation. Historical analysis allows us to trace his development over the centuries, identifying how he was reinterpreted to meet the new spiritual and political needs of the communities that worship him. Ethnography and cultural studies highlight contemporary practices involving Michael, showing how he is invoked in rituals and celebrations, as well as in the most intimate spheres of daily life, whether in family prayers or in practices of personal protection.

In a world marked by the search for a global spirituality and a return to the values of justice and protection, Michael's relevance becomes especially significant. The contemporary scenario, which combines challenges such as globalization, social crises and the expansion of digital media, creates an environment where timeless symbols, such as Michael, are reinterpreted to meet modern demands. This book seeks to contribute to a deeper understanding of how the figure of Michael responds to this growing need for connection with the spiritual and ethical, offering a point of convergence between diverse traditions.

By analyzing how Michael is invoked and reinterpreted in contemporary religious and cultural practices, the work emphasizes the persistence of symbols of protection and justice that continue to profoundly influence beliefs and behaviors. Michael's presence in movements of spiritual renewal, in popular culture, and on social media, for example, reveals that his symbolism is updated to remain relevant. He is not just a figure from the past, but an archetype that meets the needs of the present, adapting and maintaining his strength as a model of spiritual defense and moral integrity.

This study therefore seeks to situate Michael as a living symbol who not only preserves traditions but also inspires new forms of devotion and spiritual connection. He is presented as a point of convergence where human aspirations and values for justice and protection meet, demonstrating that, even in an era of rapid cultural and technological transformations, the search for archetypal figures that symbolize security, righteousness and spiritual guidance remains as relevant as in ancient times.

Analysis Methodology

To provide a truly comprehensive analysis of the figure of the Archangel Michael, this study uses an interdisciplinary approach that examines his multiple historical, cultural and contemporary dimensions. Each methodology adopted contributes to a complete and complex understanding of the way in which Michael is interpreted and venerated in different contexts and eras.

Historical analysis plays a fundamental role in tracing the origins and development of Michael's image, from its earliest mentions in religious texts to its consolidation in the Judeo-Christian and Islamic traditions. By contextualizing Michael within his historical periods, this methodology allows us to perceive how cultural, social, and religious factors shaped his character and his role within each tradition. Historical analysis is crucial to understanding the motivations underlying the representation of Michael as a divine protector and spiritual warrior. Over the centuries, changes in the interpretation of Michael's figure reflect the transformations in the spirituality and social concerns of communities, indicating that his figure is both a product and a reflection of the spiritual needs of each era.

Cultural and symbolic analysis offers a complementary dimension, focusing on the iconographic elements that define Michael's image and the spiritual meanings that these elements carry. By examining representations such as the sword, the scales, and the armor, this analysis reveals the concepts of protection, justice, and moral strength that permeate Michael's figure. The sword, for example, symbolizes truth and the ability to discern, while the scales refer to impartial justice and moral responsibility. The armor, in turn, reinforces the idea of spiritual invulnerability and defense against negative influences. The symbolic approach allows us to understand Michael as a universal archetype of defender, connecting him to similar figures in other cultures, such as divine warriors and protectors present in ancient mythologies. This connection shows that Michael represents not only a religious symbol, but a timeless human need for protection and moral integrity.

Finally, the ethnographic approach adds perspective on how Michael is received and venerated in the contemporary context.

Through interviews, case studies, and testimonies from devotees, this methodology captures Michael's vitality in modern spiritual practices. It reveals how Michael is invoked in rituals of protection and devotion, both in traditional religious contexts and in esoteric practices and new spiritualities. Furthermore, Michael's presence in digital communities shows his relevance in virtual spaces, where devotees share prayers, experiences, and guidance for invoking him. Ethnographic analysis is essential to capture how Michael continues to resonate in a scenario of spiritual diversity, offering emotional and psychological support in times of uncertainty.

The combination of these methodologies allows for a multidimensional exploration of the figure of Michael, revealing how his symbolism transcends traditional contexts and adapts to contemporary spiritual and cultural aspirations. Historical analysis provides the foundation and development of the figure of Michael, while symbolic analysis unravels the depth of his archetypal attributes. The ethnographic approach reveals Michael as an active and significant presence in modern devotional practices. Together, these methodologies provide a holistic and integrated view, highlighting Michael as an enduring archetype, essential to global spirituality, who continues to inspire and protect, both in religious traditions and in new spiritual paths emerging in contemporary society.

CHAPTER 2. ORIGINS AND FIRST MENTIONS

Historical and Religious Context

The first references to Archangel Michael are found in the three main monotheistic traditions – Judaism, Christianity and Islam – each giving him a specific role, but sharing the common denominator of protector, defender and sacred being.

In Judaism, Michael is first mentioned in the Book of Daniel as the protector of Israel and leader of the heavenly armies. Michael's designation as "one of the chief princes" positions him as the guardian not only of a people, but of the values and spiritual integrity of a nation. His role is twofold: as a warrior, he confronts the forces of evil; as a protector, he ensures the survival and justice of the people of Israel. In apocryphal texts, such as the Book of Enoch, Michael's figure is further expanded, being described as the archangel who fights the fallen angels. In this narrative, Michael becomes a defender of the divine order against the angels who corrupt humanity, reinforcing his image of righteousness and moral strength. Michael's fight against evil in Judaism symbolizes a spiritual resilience that inspires the faithful to face adversity with faith and moral purity.

In Christianity, Michael is widely recognized as the defender of good, especially in the Apocalypse (or Book of Revelation), where he leads the heavenly forces against the dragon, traditionally identified as Satan. This cosmic battle between Michael and the dragon has become one of the most powerful representations of the struggle between good and evil, consolidating Michael as the leader of the divine armies and the ultimate symbol of virtue triumphing over corruption. He not only defends heaven, but also protects the faithful against the forces of darkness. The mention of Michael in apocryphal writings and in the works of the Church Fathers reinforces his role as intercessor and protector, in addition to consolidating him as a model of virtue and justice. In Christian texts, Michael represents absolute morality and divine justice, offering the faithful an example of spiritual strength and unwavering loyalty to divine principles.

In Islam, Michael is revered as Mikail, one of the chief archangels who, alongside Jibril (Gabriel), carries out the will of God. Although his role in Islam is less military than in Judeo-Christian traditions, Mikail is still a symbol of protection and benevolence. He is depicted as a being of peace, charged with sustaining creation, dispensing divine mercy, and being responsible for rain and sustenance. Mikail's association with providence and cosmic balance differentiates him from the combative figure of Michael in Christianity, emphasizing a protection that encompasses the preservation of life and the safety of believers. This role is complemented by the deep respect accorded to him in Islam, where he is seen as a guardian who not only protects but also sustains and ensures the well-being of the faithful.

Michael's presence in these three traditions illustrates his role as a symbol of divine protection and resistance against evil, standing out as a figure of moral and spiritual strength. Michael embodies the idea of a defender of justice and order, adapting to the specificities of each tradition, but always representing integrity and the strength to resist evil. In all these traditions, he emerges as a pillar for the faithful, evoking values of courage and righteousness, and serving as a model of devotion that transcends the warrior narrative to become a guardian of faith and morality.

Comparisons with Archetypes from Other Traditions

Michael's figure as a warrior and protector finds parallels in many mythological traditions, where deities such as Mithra, Sekhmet, and Athena play similar roles as guardians and defenders. These figures not only protect their communities and ensure order, but also symbolize values such as justice, integrity, and the preservation of good, reflecting an archetypal need that spans cultures and eras.

In Persian tradition, Mithra is a deity associated with light, justice, and protection. Like Michael, he is invoked as a mediator between good and evil and is considered a defender of the just. In the Persian context, Mithra plays the role of a spiritual protector, someone who combats the forces of darkness to maintain cosmic balance. Over time, the cult of Mithra spread to the Roman Empire, where he was especially venerated by soldiers and warriors, becoming a figure of devotion for those seeking strength and protection on the battlefield. Mithra's association with the sun and the ideal of justice echoes Michael's role as a source of light and defender of divine order, showing how both figures are personifications of the struggle for good against darkness.

In Egyptian mythology, the goddess Sekhmet is a warrior and protector deity, represented as a fierce lioness. Her image is a symbol of strength and destruction, reflecting her role as the defender of Egypt against its enemies. Sekhmet was invoked to purify and fight, and her iconography, although distinct from that of Michael, bears similarities in her role as a divine protector and fighter. Both Sekhmet and Michael are seen as agents of justice, ready to destroy evil in the name of a higher order. The presence of Sekhmet as a figure of defense and combat demonstrates that the role of a divine protector, who ensures the continuity of good and the preservation of the community, is a concept that resonates in various cultures, taking forms that reflect the specificities of each tradition.

In the Greco-Roman tradition, Athena personifies wisdom and strategic warfare. Athena is venerated as a goddess who protects cities and armies, guiding warriors and ensuring the triumph of rationality and order over chaos. She is the goddess of just war, who does not engage in conflicts through violence, but rather through the maintenance of order and truth. Athena's association with the scales of justice and rational warfare reflects Michael's role as defender and guardian of divine justice. Like Michael, who represents justice and defense against evil, Athena symbolizes the ideal of ethical warfare and social and spiritual order. The connection between the two highlights a universal archetype: the sacred protector who fights in the name of truth and who is invoked to restore peace and harmony.

These comparisons between Michael, Mithra, Sekhmet, and Athena reveal that Michael's role as a warrior and protector goes beyond monotheistic traditions and is echoed in ancient mythologies from different cultures. The existence of figures of defense and justice such as these suggests a common need, deeply rooted in the collective imagination, to personify divine protection and the fight against evil. Through these figures, cultures seek a symbolic representation of a sacred protector who not only defends the community, but ensures the preservation of the values that sustain order and well-being. These archetypal figures of divine protectors reflect the universal aspiration for a being who defends good in the face of the threats of evil, connecting traditions around a shared ideal of security, righteousness, and justice.

Michael as a Universal Archetype

From a Jungian perspective, Michael can be understood as a universal archetype, a symbol that emerges from the collective unconscious and carries with it deep and timeless themes of protection, justice and resistance to evil. According to Carl Jung, archetypes are primordial patterns common to all humanity, manifesting themselves in myths, religions and cultural narratives, regardless of time and space. Michael, representing the "protective hero", is one of these universal archetypes that embodies the value of fighting against dark forces, a symbol that goes beyond physical combat to reflect a spiritual and psychological battle for the integrity of the human soul.

As a protective hero, Michael stands out as a figure who responds to the human need for safety and security, especially in times of uncertainty and conflict. He is invoked not only as a defender against external battles, but also as a guardian against internal struggles, acting as a spiritual support for those facing fears, doubts, and threats to their moral integrity. Michael's duality—his fighting strength combined with deep compassion—resonates broadly with the human search for comfort and security in the face of the unknown. His image offers a sense of stability, representing both the power to repel evil and the ideal of a sustaining presence.

The archetype of Michael thus transcends the boundaries of specific religions, acting as a universal symbol of order and spiritual protection. This archetype reflects the human desire for a defender who can restore order amid chaos and ensure justice amid uncertainty. The image of Michael is echoed in various global religious and mythological traditions, where similar figures emerge as protectors and agents of justice, often symbolizing the triumph of light over shadows and truth over falsehood. These figures, like Michael, act as archetypal responses to the human struggle for ethical and moral survival, offering a sense of cosmic order and rescuing values of integrity and righteousness.

Thus, the invocation of Michael as defender and protector meets a common archetypal need to seek strength that can combat the "shadows" — whether internal or external. His figure represents the triumph of good over evil and justice over injustice, providing a reference of moral strength and protection that strengthens individuals in their spiritual and psychological journeys. He is not only a symbol of protection; he is also a projection of the human desire for universal support, which ensures order and goodness amidst life's adversities. In this way, Michael is configured as an integrating archetype, capable of uniting people around a common struggle to defend the essential values of existence, reflecting a need that transcends cultures and religions, establishing himself as a timeless symbol of light, truth and spiritual security.

CHAPTER 3. NARRATIVES AND LEGENDS

The Battle Against Evil

The legendary battle between Archangel Michael and Satan is one of the most iconic and powerful narratives in the Christian tradition, highlighting him as the supreme protector of good and the tireless fighter against the forces of evil. In the Apocalypse (or Book of Revelation), the image of Michael leading the heavenly armies against the dragon, symbol of Satan, takes on a central role, illustrating the cosmic battle between good and evil. In this confrontation, Satan seeks to usurp the divine throne, while Michael, as a celestial warrior, fights to maintain divine order and justice, defending the integrity of heaven and, symbolically, of the spiritual world.

Described as an event of apocalyptic proportions, this battle is more than a physical struggle; it represents the final victory of light over darkness and the triumph of truth and justice over falsehood and corruption. By driving the dragon and his followers from heaven, Michael asserts himself as the supreme defender not only of the heavens but also of the faithful. This narrative serves to cement his position in the Christian imagination as an armed and determined angel whose mission is to repel all that threatens peace and order. The image of Michael subduing Satan has become an iconic visual symbol of the triumph of good over evil and the inevitability of divine justice, inspiring artistic representations over the centuries, from frescoes to monumental sculptures, that convey the idea of an unbeatable defender and a justice that prevails.

The impact of this narrative goes beyond religious literature. It establishes Michael as a symbol of hope and victory, especially in times of crisis and uncertainty. Believers and devotees see Michael's battle as a metaphor for personal and collective struggles against forces that threaten spiritual and moral integrity. The figure of Michael as an active protector, who does not hesitate to confront evil, offers a source of inspiration and courage, encouraging devotees to maintain their faith and resist adversity with confidence. The representation of Michael in action against Satan reinforces the idea that good, even when faced with great challenges, has the strength and determination to prevail.

This legend reinforces Michael's warrior character, underscoring his role as a constant defender of light and truth. He not only confronts evil, but banishes it, reaffirming the principle that divine justice is unshakable and infallible. In the religious imagination, Michael is more than an angel: he is the tireless protector who does not allow destructive forces to prosper. He symbolizes absolute courage and commitment to divine order, offering devotees a sense of security and protection in times of doubt and spiritual distress. Through his image, Michael's narrative becomes a lasting legacy, cementing his role as protector of faith and pillar of hope for those facing the uncertainties of spiritual life.

Other Narratives and Associated Stories

The figure of Archangel Michael is a richly complex one, composed of symbolic and narrative layers that transcend the simple image of a celestial warrior to become a total protector—one who not only combats destructive forces but also acts as a compassionate defender, intercessor, and symbol of spiritual harmony. Each of the religious traditions that include Michael in their theology offers a unique and detailed view of his attributes and roles, contributing to a multifaceted understanding that goes far beyond the concept of an angel armed against evil.

In the Book of Enoch, an apocryphal text central to both early Judaism and early Christianity, Michael is described as the chief commander of the heavenly forces against the rebellion of the fallen angels. These angels, led by figures such as Azazel and Semjaza, are said to have disobeyed divine order by corrupting humanity, sharing forbidden knowledge, and leading people astray from spiritual purity. Michael's responsibility here is twofold: he must restore order in the spiritual world and, at the same time, purify humanity from the corrupting effects of this rebellion. Michael, therefore, is more than a warrior; he is a purifier and a restorer of the divine order. His fight against these fallen angels is not just a physical battle, but a moral struggle, requiring a defender of absolute integrity, one who refuses to allow corruption to penetrate the divine order and contaminate the good. Michael's role here symbolizes the eternal need to rebalance forces and maintain spiritual purity, offering humanity a path back to justice and harmony.

Within the Talmud and rabbinic Jewish tradition, Michael is given a treatment that emphasizes his status as an intercessor and protector of humanity. He is seen not only as a warrior, but also as a defender and mediator, someone who acts to protect the righteous and the innocent and intercedes for those in need. This role for Michael reinforces an image of mercy and care, highlighting him as an intermediary between humanity and God, someone who is constantly vigilant to ensure that the prayers of the righteous are heard. In several Talmudic stories and passages, Michael appears as one who advocates on behalf of human beings, fighting evil at deep and subtle levels. His role is both a barrier against destructive forces and a moral support for those facing challenges. He thus becomes a symbol of ongoing protection, a heavenly being who not only shields humanity from external threats, but who also acts to strengthen the righteous internally, reinforcing their virtues and encouraging them to live ethical and godly lives.

In Islamic tradition, Mikail (corresponding to Michael) is revered in a way that highlights his role as a dispenser of divine mercy and blessing. Mikail is associated with maintaining cosmic balance, responsible for providing rain, fertility and sustenance to creation. This role represents a fundamental aspect of harmony and benevolence, where Mikail not only cares for humanity in a physical sense, but also ensures that the means of subsistence are always available. He is seen as an angel of peace and prosperity, acting to preserve life and maintain the well-being of creation. Instead of a figure of direct combat against evil, Mikail appears as a guardian of universal harmony, whose role is to guarantee the continuity of life in peace and the maintenance of the natural order. His image offers a balanced view of Michael, who, alongside his warrior aspect, also has a face of deep compassion and care for divine creation, reflecting the aspect of a protector who actively cares about the prosperity and stability of the world.

These narratives reveal an additional depth to Michael, one that goes beyond the sword-wielding, armor-clad warrior. He represents a type of force that is both combative and restorative, an agent of divine justice whose presence not only wards off evil but also promotes well-being and harmony. In many mystical and esoteric traditions, Michael is seen as a spiritual guide who helps devotees overcome inner fears and emotional conflicts, representing the light that combats inner shadows. His image serves as a mirror for those facing personal and spiritual challenges, encouraging a search for self-knowledge and self-improvement. Michael, while protecting against external forces, invites the faithful to confront their own limitations and seek the truth within themselves.

Furthermore, this multiplicity of roles reveals Michael as a figure of moral and spiritual support for his devotees, providing a sense of security that transcends the physical struggle against evil. He is seen as a celestial being who offers comfort and strengthens the faith of those who turn to him. In moments of despair and doubt, Michael's presence is invoked as a source of hope and security, a protector who not only defends but also nourishes the soul. His actions are symbolic and practical, responding to both the deep spiritual needs and the daily appeals of the faithful. This makes him an archetype of strength, compassion, and justice, a being who adapts to the needs of each moment and each individual, offering a comprehensive response to life's challenges.

Cultural Variations in Legends

Michael's image as defender and protector has a unique capacity for adaptation, allowing him to take on characteristics that fit a wide range of cultural and historical contexts. This flexibility not only increases his relevance, but also establishes him as a symbol of universal protection, shaped according to the specific needs and values of each society. From medieval Europe to the cultures of Latin America and Middle Eastern communities, Michael appears in many different forms, each reflecting the cultural and spiritual nuances of those places.

In medieval Europe, the figure of Michael was fundamental in the construction of the ethic of chivalry and the ideal of the Christian knight. With the fervor of the Crusades and the intense religiosity that permeated the Middle Ages, Michael was transformed into a kind of divine knight, a model of righteousness and courage. During this period, he was widely invoked as the patron saint of battles and defender of the faith. Michael was seen as a supreme example for Christian warriors, whose mission went beyond physical combat, encompassing an ideal of fighting for divine justice and protecting the innocent. Thus, he became an icon in the construction of the code of conduct of chivalry, representing virtues such as loyalty, bravery and devotion. Michael was not just an angel; he was an ideal of Christian life. In paintings, statues and prayers, his image inspired leaders and soldiers, who found in him a moral and spiritual guide to face their challenges in the name of faith.

In Latin America, Miguel's presence is adapted and enriched with elements of indigenous traditions and popular religiosity. In particular, in Mexican traditions, it is often associated with popular rituals and festivities that combine indigenous and Christian aspects. In these celebrations, Miguel is invoked as a protector of homes and families, someone who has the power to ward off evil spirits and negative influences. This vision of Miguel as guardian of personal and family spaces resonates deeply in communities, where he is seen as a powerful saint, capable of ensuring the peace and well-being of those who invoke him. These celebrations, which often include processions and dances, represent a fusion of spiritualities, in which Miguel is not only a Christian archangel, but also a local protector, adapted to the values and beliefs of Latin American culture. His figure symbolizes hope and resilience, especially in communities that have historically faced social and economic challenges, reinforcing Miguel's role as a source of strength and resistance.

In the Middle East, Michael is widely venerated by both Christians and Muslims, especially in communities experiencing conflict and adversity. Here, he is seen as a symbol of resilience, peace, and unity. In regions where calamities and political tensions are constant, the invocation of Michael takes on the character of a plea for protection and stability. For many, he represents a force that transcends religious divisions, an angel who protects and intercedes in times of need, regardless of belief or origin. In the mystical traditions of Islam, especially in Sufism, Michael (or Mikail) is revered in prayers and supplications that ask for protection, prosperity, and harmony. Here, he symbolizes the capacity for spiritual preservation and security, an angel who offers peace in a world marked by instability. This mystical reverence reflects Michael's ability to adapt to the deep spiritual yearnings of the local culture, offering support that is simultaneously spiritual and moral.

These cultural variations demonstrate the incredible resilience and plasticity of Michael's image. He adapts to the historical and spiritual contexts of each community, not only being reinterpreted but also resignified to meet the particular needs of each group. In all these traditions, he symbolizes a universal defender, a protector who transcends cultural and religious barriers, serving as a point of convergence for diverse human aspirations. Michael's malleability allows him to resonate with different anxieties and hopes, from internal and spiritual struggles to material conflicts and battles, which explains his longevity as a symbol of protection and justice.

This flexibility also allows Michael to be a living symbol, responsive to changing times and circumstances, ensuring his continued relevance. He is a figure who provides emotional, spiritual, and cultural security to his devotees, adjusting himself to meet their specific needs, whether as a divine knight, a guardian of homes, or a protector against calamity. The resilience of his image, which unites societies and religious traditions around a common archetype of defense and justice, highlights his importance not only as a religious figure, but as a timeless symbol that embodies the human search for protection, integrity, and stability in an ever-changing world.

CHAPTER 4. SYMBOLISM AND ICONOGRAPHY

Artistic Representations of Miguel

Artistic depictions of Archangel Michael throughout the centuries express his role as supreme defender of good, imbuing him with a visual force that not only inspires but also communicates a powerful spiritual narrative. From Byzantine mosaics and icons to Renaissance and neoclassical paintings, the figure of Michael has been a constant, adapting to the different aesthetics and values of each period, but always preserving his essence as an angelic warrior and guardian of divine justice.

During the Renaissance, a period marked by the rebirth of the arts and a focus on idealized beauty and heroic strength, Michael was depicted by great masters such as Guido Reni, Raphael, and Michelangelo, who shaped the classical iconography of the archangel. These depictions often show him armed with a sword and wearing armor, defeating demons or a dragon, reinforcing the image of Michael as a symbol of unshakable virtue and sacred power. His figure conveys a combination of angelic beauty and invincible strength, encapsulating the Renaissance vision of a spirituality that is at once aesthetic and uplifting.

Guido Reni, in his famous work "Saint Michael the Archangel" (c. 1635), elevated Michael to an icon of serenity and angelic majesty. In the painting, Michael stands over the fallen devil, with an expression of calm and absolute control, conveying a sense of strength and purity. The contrast between light and shadow is used to emphasize his position as guardian of good, highlighting the beauty of his figure as a reflection of his holiness and divine authority. This representation became a reference for later generations, being repeated in several churches and cathedrals throughout Europe, consolidating the image of Michael as a symbol of spiritual strength and moral perfection.

In his work "Saint Michael and the Dragon," Raphael presents Michael in a more dynamic posture, capturing the archangel in full combat. Raphael opts for a composition that emphasizes the movement and intensity of the combat, making Michael's determination and energy in the fight against evil evident. Michael's expression and the dramatic positioning of his body highlight the urgency and seriousness of his mission as a defender of good. This representation emphasizes

Michael's active nature, highlighting him as a warrior in action, who not only contemplates justice, but vigorously applies it against evil.

Michelangelo, in the iconic Sistine Chapel fresco, creates a representation of Michael that combines his role as a warrior with that of a judge. Amidst the apocalyptic context of the Last Judgment, Michael appears as a figure who watches over divine order, ready to maintain justice against chaos and destructive forces. In Michelangelo's vision, Michael is not just a fighter; he is the cosmic guardian, whose authority encompasses moral judgment and the role of protector. This representation places Michael in a scenario of universal scope, reinforcing his role in maintaining balance and divine justice.

Depictions of Michael over the centuries have not been limited to the Renaissance. In earlier periods, such as the Byzantine Empire, Michael was widely depicted in mosaics and icons, where his image was stylized with rigid features and an expression of heavenly authority. In Byzantine icons, Michael is often shown frontally, with a formal and static posture, expressing a strength that is more contemplative and stable. These mosaics sought to convey the idea of Michael as a constant protective presence, someone who observes and ensures the divine order in a solemn and unyielding manner.

Later, in the Baroque, Miguel was again reinterpreted in sculptures and paintings that emphasized the drama and movement characteristic of the time. The baroque representations of Miguel are marked by a grandeur that captures the moment of his victory over evil in impressive detail, intensifying the emotion and tension of the scene. This baroque vision of Miguel accentuates his strength and bravery, while engaging the viewer in an almost theatrical experience of triumph and justice.

In Neoclassicism, Michael was portrayed with a sobriety that returned to classical influences, maintaining Michael's image as a symbol of heroic virtue and heavenly order, but with an aesthetic of balance and simplicity. These representations are more restrained, highlighting Miguel as a defender who, above all, represents a high form of morality and spiritual balance.

The diversity of styles and interpretations across artistic periods reveals that Michael's image is timeless and malleable, capable of being reinterpreted to suit the specific aspirations and values of each era. In each period, he is reshaped to reflect what society considers the ideal embodiment of virtue, courage, and justice. At the same time, this continuity of representations maintains Michael's essence as a figure of light and spiritual protection, offering devotees and spectators a constant reference of security and hope. Michael's iconography, with his sword, armor, and imposing posture, influences the perception of the faithful, who find in him an example of righteousness and an unbreakable source of spiritual inspiration.

Symbol Meanings (Sword, Scales, Armor)

The symbolic elements associated with Archangel Michael – the sword, the scales and the armor – play central roles in the construction of his image as defender of the divine order and judge of souls. Each symbol contributes to a multifaceted vision of Miguel, which combines the role of warrior and protector with the role of moral judge, reflecting the complexity of his spiritual mission.

The Sword

Michael's sword is a powerful symbol that carries multiple spiritual meanings, being an instrument of truth and divine justice. As a warrior archangel, Michael uses the sword not only to defeat evil in its physical form, but also to represent the power of discernment that separates good from evil. In Christian iconography, the sword is often positioned pointing downward, resting on the dragon or evil forces, suggesting its victory and supremacy over evil. This gesture indicates that evil has been subdued and that Michael is an agent of purification, using the sword to cut through and drive away the darkness and restore divine order.

Furthermore, Michael's sword carries a moral and spiritual dimension: it represents truth that cuts through falsehood and righteousness that rejects corruption. In esoteric and mystical contexts, the sword is seen as an extension of the divine force that grants Michael the power to protect and purify, not only externally but also internally, encouraging the faithful to reflect on their own moral struggles and the search for truth in their lives. The sword, therefore, is not just a symbol of physical strength; it is an emblem of moral authority and divine judgment, reminding the faithful that good, represented by Michael, always prevails over darkness.

The Scale

The scales that Michael holds in some depictions add a dimension of divine judgment and impartiality to his figure. A universal symbol of justice, the scales represent the ability to weigh souls, examining the morality and actions of individuals to determine their spiritual destiny. In the context of the final judgment, the scales symbolize Michael's role as judge, emphasizing that he is not only a combatant against the forces of evil, but also an arbiter who ensures that each soul's destiny is aligned with divine justice.

Michael's scales carry a strong moral charge, reminding the faithful that every action and choice made during life will have a spiritual weight and consequence. The image of Michael with the scales reinforces the ideal of moral rectitude and ethical responsibility, encouraging the faithful to live in accordance with spiritual values. In medieval and Renaissance iconography, the scales also became a pedagogical tool, used to teach the value of an ethical life and the idea that there will be a judgment where divine justice will be applied in a ruthless and equitable manner. Michael, as the bearer of the scales, assumes the role of a judge who not only combats external evil, but also evaluates the purity of souls, highlighting the importance of a life guided by justice.

The Armor

Miguel's armor is one of the most visually striking and symbolically rich elements in his iconography. Representing protection and invulnerability, the armor shines as a reflection of the holiness and divine strength that surrounds Michael. It symbolizes the invincibility of good and spiritual fortitude, suggesting that Miguel is immune to the temptations and attacks of evil. Armor is not just combat equipment, but a visual statement that purity and holiness are inviolable and unshakable.

For the faithful, Michael's armor serves as an invitation to cultivate their own spiritual fortitude, a moral and ethical resilience against adversity. On a deeper level, the armor represents the divine protection he extends to the faithful, assuring them safety in times of crisis and encouraging them to clothe themselves with virtues that can strengthen them. This metaphor is powerful: Michael's armor not only defends against external evils, but inspires a kind of inner invulnerability, motivating the faithful to stand firm in their spiritual convictions and resist the negative influences of the world.

The Combination of Symbols

The interplay of these three symbols—sword, scales, and armor—creates a holistic image of Michael as defender, judge, and spiritual guardian. Each symbol reinforces an aspect of Michael's mission, and together they build a complete representation of his divine role. He is at once a fearless warrior who combats evil forces, an impartial judge who weighs souls, and an unwavering protector who offers spiritual security. This triad of symbols connects Michael to a series of spiritual and moral values that are passed on to the faithful, reminding them of the importance of seeking truth, living justly, and protecting themselves from destructive influences.

These symbols also transcend their aesthetic function to communicate a profound spiritual message. The sword, scales, and armor serve as archetypal emblems of protection and justice, inspiring devotees to see Michael not simply as an angelic figure, but as an ideal of moral strength and purity. Each element functions as a part of Michael's legacy, influencing devotion to him and serving as a visual reminder of his protective presence and his mission to ensure divine order amidst chaos.

Michael's iconography, then, is not merely decorative; it is a powerful vehicle for communicating the spiritual principles of protection, justice, and holiness. The sword calls for the struggle for truth, the scales call for justice and righteousness, and the armor represents the security and refuge offered by faith. These symbols make Michael a figure not only of worship but also of inspiration and role model, conveying a message of courage, protection, and moral integrity that has resonated deeply in the hearts of believers throughout the centuries.

Miguel in Classical Art and Religious Heritage

Miguel's presence in religious heritage is a concrete manifestation of his spiritual function, expressed in artistic representations that, in addition to beautifying the sacred space, create a visual and symbolic connection between devotees and the divine world. These representations range from imposing cathedrals to small chapels, and over the centuries have become tangible symbols of Michael's protection and power. In each context, Michael is portrayed in a way that reflects not only his angelic identity but also the spiritual aspirations of the community that venerates him.

In Gothic cathedrals, Michael is often integrated into the architecture as a guardian of the temple and a protector of the faith. Gothic architecture itself, with its soaring spires and detailed facades that point toward the heavens, suggests a direct connection with the divine. Michael is depicted as a watchful defender, positioned at the entrances, towers, or main facades of cathedrals, acting as a protective figure who symbolically repels the forces of evil and ensures peace within the sacred space. Michael's position in Gothic cathedrals is not accidental; he is strategically placed, as if defending the temple against spiritual invaders, highlighting his role as guardian of spaces dedicated to faith and devotion. This presence of Michael in Gothic architecture not only communicates protection, but also inspires a sense of awe and security in the faithful, who see him as a symbol of heavenly resistance and security.

In the Byzantine tradition, Michael is widely represented in mosaics that adorn the walls and vaults of ancient churches. Byzantine mosaics are characterized by an aesthetic of great austerity and solemnity, which reinforces the image of Michael as a figure of spiritual authority. In these mosaics, Michael is depicted in a formal manner, with rigid facial features and a countenance that exudes strength and serenity. This style of representation reflects Byzantine theology, which valued the transcendence and majesty of sacred figures. Michael, therefore, appears as an imposing guardian of the divine order, a constant and protective presence who ensures the spiritual integrity of the church and its devotees. The austerity of the mosaics does not seek to humanize Michael, but rather to emphasize his role as a celestial being whose function is to ensure that the sacred remains inviolate.

Stained glass windows in medieval churches offer another powerful interpretation of Michael's image, depicting him in scenes of the Last Judgment, where he weighs souls and judges their actions. These stained glass windows, with their vibrant colors and dramatic scenes, were a form of visual catechesis for the faithful, many of whom were illiterate. The image of Michael weighing souls served as a constant reminder of the importance of moral rectitude and divine judgment. Michael appears not only as a warrior, but as a compassionate and impartial judge, whose scales ensure that each soul is treated according to its purity and virtues. These stained glass windows were carefully positioned to catch the sunlight, creating an aura of holiness around Michael and reinforcing his role as a figure of justice and truth, able to guide the faithful on their spiritual journey.

In addition to large structures, Michael is also present in Orthodox reliquaries and icons, especially in Eastern Christian churches. Icons of Michael are revered as sacred objects, used in prayers and ceremonies that invoke his protection. In Orthodox iconography, he is depicted with calm seriousness, often holding a sword or spear, symbols of his role as a warrior against evil. Icons of Michael transcend mere artistic value; they are considered windows to the spiritual world, channels through which the faithful can connect with Michael's protective and compassionate presence. Through icons, devotees encounter an image of Michael that not only protects them, but also brings them closer to the divine, reinforcing their trust in heavenly protection.

In many parts of the world, Michael is also the patron saint of churches, cities, and communities, a tradition that symbolizes collective trust in the strength and protection he provides. Celebrations in his honor, such as patronal feasts and processions, reinforce this public devotion and demonstrate Michael's importance as a symbol of hope and resilience. In many communities, especially in Europe and Latin America, festivities dedicated to Michael are held to celebrate his role as a protector against evil, integrating them into local traditions and reinforcing his place in the daily lives of devotees. These festivities and tributes are more than religious rituals; they are a reaffirmation of Michael's role as guardian of the collective faith, a defender who, according to popular belief, remains vigilant in times of prosperity and adversity.

Over the centuries, Michael's iconography in a variety of artistic styles and forms—from sculptures and mosaics to stained glass and icons—has cemented his image as a constant and protective presence in the spiritual life of communities. Each representation, adapted to the style and needs of its time, functions as a visual expression of Michael as moral guide, defender, and judge. For the faithful, these works of art go beyond their aesthetic value; they are instruments of faith, reinforcing the protection and spiritual support that Michael offers. Ultimately, these artistic representations bring Michael closer to the devotees, offering a tangible presence that strengthens devotion and inspires trust, creating a link between the visible and invisible worlds and making Michael an eternal figure of courage, justice, and protection.

CHAPTER 5. SPIRITUAL AND PHILOSOPHICAL ROLE

Michael as Protector and Divine Warrior

Archangel Michael occupies a fundamental and universal role as protector and defender of the righteous, a figure who transcends religious traditions and resonates with a wide variety of spiritual contexts. His image as a divine warrior positions him as a symbol of protection, courage, and strength, qualities that make him an inspiring presence for those seeking spiritual safety amid danger and adversity. Michael is not just an angelic figure; he represents the struggle to preserve sacred order, acting as a barrier against the chaotic and destructive forces that threaten divine harmony.

In Christian tradition, Michael is seen as the defender of the Church and the guardian of God's people. Since the early centuries of Christianity, he has been invoked in prayers and rituals of protection, being celebrated as a tireless fighter against evil and a powerful figure of intercession. Michael's role goes beyond physical defense, as he is also considered the guardian of souls, ensuring that evil is warded off and that divine justice prevails. In many prayers and litanies, Michael is remembered as the "prince of the heavenly host", a reference to his command over the heavenly armies and his mission to protect the faithful from evil influences. His presence is seen as a support for Christians, who trust in his protection for both the community and their individual spiritual lives. Devotion to Michael reflects the desire for spiritual security and the trust in divine strength as a real and tangible protection.

Miguel's role as a defender is not limited to the Christian context, it also finds an echo in Islam. In Islamic traditions, Mikail (the equivalent of Michael) is revered as a symbol of mercy and preservation of creation. Although the emphasis is not on the direct fight against evil, Mikail is associated with maintaining cosmic balance and providing sustenance, representing continuous support and a force that maintains the harmony of creation. Mikail is seen as a serene and compassionate presence, someone who protects believers by ensuring that divine blessings are constantly renewed and distributed. Thus, while Michael in Christianity is more often portrayed as a warrior and a judge, Mikail embodies a protection that manifests itself in the preservation and sustenance of life, reflecting a complementary vision of protection that encompasses both the physical and the spiritual.

The figure of Michael, with his role as a divine warrior, transcends cultural and religious boundaries, uniting different traditions around a common ideal of protection and spiritual courage. As an archangel, Michael inspires unshakable confidence amid life's struggles and challenges, reminding his devotees that there is a greater force at work, committed to defending good and upholding justice. His role goes beyond personal protection; he represents the security that each devotee seeks when facing the uncertainties and dangers of the world. Michael not only wards off evil, but also instills a sense of courage, encouraging his faithful to remain steadfast and dedicate themselves to a life of righteousness and moral integrity, regardless of adversity.

Michael's protective function reflects an archetypal human need for safety and support in the midst of chaos, which is why he is so powerful and widely revered. Throughout the generations, he has been invoked as a watchful presence and a symbol of hope for those facing trials. In times of uncertainty, Michael's image brings deep comfort, offering the assurance that there is an eternal and incorruptible guardian committed to preserving the good and supporting his devotees. In this way, Michael establishes himself as a universal figure of spiritual defense, inspiring devotees to resist negative forces and to believe in divine protection that transcends any adversity.

In short, Michael is an icon of courage, protection, and justice, an angelic being who symbolizes the spiritual ideal of defending good and divine order. In all traditions that revere him, Michael is a figure who not only protects but also motivates and inspires, offering devotees a clear example of perseverance and spiritual determination. He is a guardian who maintains security and justice amidst the challenges of the world, and his role transcends the physical plane, operating in the spiritual realm to ensure that the principles of good, truth, and sacred order prevail.

Ethical and Moral Implications

Archangel Michael transcends the role of a simple celestial warrior to become a symbol of justice and ethical responsibility. His figure evokes profound themes of morality, portraying an ideal of protection that goes beyond the physical defense of the righteous and involves an ethical and spiritual responsibility towards the divine order. The image of Michael invites us to reflect on what it truly means to defend the good, highlighting the idea of a justice that is firm, impartial and committed to the preservation of moral and spiritual integrity.

In the Christian tradition, Michael is more than a fighter; he is a judge and executor of divine justice. This role entails a moral responsibility that requires maintaining universal order and defending the values of truth and righteousness. As "prince of the heavenly host," Michael acts as an agent of divine justice, charged with discerning between good and evil and applying the appropriate consequences to each. This aspect of Michael not only exalts strength and protection, but promotes a vision of justice that is relentless in the face of evil, serving as an example to the faithful of the importance of defending what is morally right, regardless of adversity.

Michael's ethical role is thus an invitation to moral reflection for the devout. He acts not out of personal motivations but as a representative of the universal order, a being who symbolizes justice that remains faithful to truth. Michael, as an angelic figure, offers a model of transcendental ethics, suggesting that the struggle against evil is ultimately a battle for the preservation of the divine order. This aspect of his personality inspires believers to align their own lives with a standard of morality that values the collective good above individual interests. Michael thus becomes a spiritual guide for those who seek to live a life of righteousness, encouraging them to defend good and resist evil, even when facing evil requires courage and sacrifice.

Philosophically, Michael's role can be interpreted in light of the concept of distributive justice and the responsibility to protect the vulnerable. Michael's justice is impartial and absolute, symbolizing the notion that evil must be combated so that good can thrive. In philosophical traditions, justice is often seen as a central principle that ensures the cohesion and peace of society. Michael, by combating evil and protecting the good, reflects a conception of justice that is intrinsically linked to the duty to preserve social and spiritual balance. His role as defender of the just and guardian of the innocent echoes an ethical responsibility that is as relevant in theology as it is in theories of human justice. His struggle is a fundamental moral responsibility, a demonstration that the defense of good and resistance to evil are central principles of coexistence and universal order.

Furthermore, Michael represents an ethical struggle that resonates in today's social and spiritual contexts. By protecting the innocent and combating evil, Michael becomes a model of active advocacy, inspiring believers to adopt a stance of protection and justice in their own lives and communities. In a social context, Michael's image encourages people to be agents of change and advocates for the vulnerable, fostering a commitment to justice that goes beyond words and manifests itself in concrete actions. For believers, Michael represents the idea that defending the good is a moral imperative, and that each individual has an ethical responsibility to act as a guardian of truth and justice in his or her own circle.

The image of Michael also reminds us that protecting the good is not a passive task, but a mission that requires courage, discipline, and determination. He inspires devotees to act justly and to protect their values in the face of difficulties, demonstrating that the fight for good is an active responsibility that demands commitment and dedication. His figure transcends the religious dimension, promoting an ethical ideal that extends to the daily lives of the faithful and aligns with the notions of social responsibility and moral justice. In Michael, we find an archetype of moral strength and defense of justice that inspires devotees to be courageous, upright, and resilient, assuming the responsibility of protecting and preserving the good in their own lives and in society.

Thus, Archangel Michael represents an ideal of universal justice and ethics, which encourages each individual to be a defender of good and a fighter against evil, both on a personal and collective level. He is a symbol of moral courage and a source of inspiration for those who seek to live a life of righteousness and protection of the most vulnerable. The figure of Michael, therefore, not only elevates spirituality, but also promotes values that are fundamental to ethical coexistence and the construction of a just society, where good is protected and evil is resisted with firmness and compassion.

Psychology and Spirituality

In psychology, especially in Jungian theory, Archangel Michael can be understood as an archetypal symbol of inner courage and facing one's inner "shadows," a central concept in Carl Jung's work. According to Jung, figures like Michael represent the archetype of the hero, a character who emerges in narratives and mythologies as one who is willing to face the challenging and dark forces that reside in the human unconscious. This hero is not only a physical fighter, but also a symbol of higher aspects of the self that fight for integrity, morality, and personal development. Michael, then, becomes a guide for those who seek to overcome personal fears and limitations, inviting each one to explore the depths of their own psyche and confront repressed or neglected elements.

The narrative of Michael's battle against Satan, described in the Book of Revelation, can be interpreted through this lens as a metaphor for the confrontation between the dark and light aspects of the human psyche. In this context, Michael represents the "light of consciousness" that opposes destructive and unconscious forces, symbolizing the process by which the individual seeks to overcome negative traits and reconcile with internal impulses and conflicts. Michael therefore personifies the struggle for self-transformation and alignment with ethical principles and high values, fundamental elements for a life of balance and spiritual fulfillment. This process, known in psychology as "individuation," is the path that Jung describes for the integration of the dark aspects and the achievement of inner unity. Thus, by confronting and mastering the "dragon" or "devil" within, the individual approaches a more complete and whole version of himself, in an ongoing journey of self-knowledge.

In addition to being a symbol of the inner struggle for integrity, the figure of Michael is also a source of inspiration and resilience for those facing external crises and challenges. In devotional and spiritual practices, many invoke Michael in times of difficulty, seeking his protection against both tangible dangers and psychological and emotional threats. In psychology, this invocation of Michael can be understood as a process of mobilizing one's own inner strengths, where the image of the warrior archangel helps the individual to access his own courage and deal with emotional and psychological problems with greater security. Michael, as a spiritual warrior, acts as a projection of human capacities for perseverance and overcoming, encouraging devotees to find within themselves the strength to confront their own anxieties and fears.

The spirituality associated with Michael promotes a journey of self-knowledge and self-improvement, where each devotee is encouraged to face their inner shadows and seek a state of enlightenment and inner peace. This journey of spiritual and psychological growth requires courage and honesty with oneself, and Michael, as a spiritual guide, represents the energy needed to deal with this task. He not only protects against external threats, but also helps the devotee to face their own conflicts and vulnerabilities, offering guidance that promotes moral and spiritual growth. This process is aligned with the practice of introspection and meditation, where the individual, inspired by the image of Michael, is invited to investigate their emotions, their insecurities and to confront destructive impulses, transforming them into strength and wisdom.

Jung described confronting one's inner shadows as an inevitable and often painful but necessary challenge for personal transformation. The figure of Michael provides a symbolic and archetypal framework that facilitates this process, allowing individuals to visualize and understand their own inner struggle as part of a larger narrative. Michael represents spiritual security and the desire for a life aligned with deep values, but he also symbolizes the effort required to achieve these ideals. He encourages devotees to face their own limitations and to strengthen their inner "armor" against negative influences, fostering a self-confidence that is cultivated through self-knowledge and the pursuit of righteousness.

On the deepest level, Miguel is an archetypal spiritual and moral guide, a defender of integrity who stands alongside those who seek to live ethically and authentically. He teaches that the fight for light and truth begins within each person, and that true spiritual protection comes from the courage to face one's shadows and seek a life of harmony and balance. In this way, Miguel is not just a protector, but a symbol of personal transformation that challenges the individual to align with what is highest and most integral in their being.

CHAPTER 6. THE RELEVANCE OF MICHAEL OVER THE CENTURIES

Antiquity and Mythological Cultures

Throughout antiquity, many cultures incorporated mythological figures who assumed the role of protectors, warriors, and guardians of cosmic balance, and who have significant parallels with Archangel Michael. These figures not only reflect Michael's role, but have also influenced his image and symbolism in Western traditions, forming a web of meanings and archetypes that transcend cultural and religious barriers. This common imagery of a defender of good reveals an archetypal human need for security and protection against the forces of chaos and destruction.

In Zoroastrianism, the god Mithra is a striking example of a being who, like Michael, is associated with the preservation of order and the fight against the forces of darkness. Mithra was venerated as an intermediary between the earthly and divine worlds, occupying the role of guardian of light and justice. In his depictions, he appears as a combatant of darkness and a defender of cosmic integrity, characteristics that resonate deeply with the image of Michael as defender of good and guardian of the celestial order. Mithra symbolizes the divine light that combats darkness and ensures the protection of the righteous, a role that echoes in Michael's function as leader of the heavenly armies and defender of the faith. The reverence for Mithra, which later spread throughout the Roman Empire, demonstrates that the notion of a protective warrior was deeply rooted in ancient societies and directly influenced the symbolic construction of protective figures in Western monotheistic traditions.

In Egyptian mythology, the goddess Sekhmet also plays a role that echoes Michael's functions, despite cultural and gender differences. Sekhmet, represented as a lioness, is a deity associated with power and protection, and is invoked to ensure victory and protect the pharaoh in battle. She is not only a figure of physical strength, but also a symbol of the defense of order and morality, where her destructive power is balanced by a responsibility to preserve good. Like Michael, who acts as a purifier by fighting evil, Sekhmet is seen as a goddess whose fury has a moral and purifying function, aimed at preserving harmony. Although Michael is usually represented as a male figure and Sekhmet as a female goddess, both share the role of warriors who exercise justice and spiritual protection. Their image as protectors suggests that the need for a being who defends good, eliminating evil forces, is a constant in the human psyche, adapted to the cultural specificities of each society.

Another significant parallel is found in Greek mythology, with the goddess Athena, who combines attributes of wisdom, military strategy, and justice. Athena is revered as a goddess who protects cities and warriors, embodying both skill in combat and a commitment to order and righteousness. Athena acts as a defender of communities and ethical values, a role that resonates with Michael's role as defender of faith and the community of believers in Christianity. Both are symbols of a "just protector" who fights evil not out of hatred, but to defend justice and maintain peace. Athena, with her spear and shield, reflects wisdom in war and a commitment to justice, elements that also characterize Michael, especially in his role as judge and warrior against dark forces. Athena's presence in Greek mythology demonstrates a universality of the just protector archetype, which transcends cultures and is rooted in the human need for spiritual leaders and figures who ensure order.

These mythological figures from antiquity reveal that the image of Michael as a divine warrior and defender of good did not emerge in isolation, but is part of a collective and ancestral imagination that crosses cultural and religious boundaries. The archetype of the "defender of good" manifests a human search for protection and security against the destructive forces that threaten the integrity of the world and the community. Over time, this archetype was absorbed and adapted by Western monotheistic traditions, especially in Christianity, where Michael became the celestial warrior who defends the faith and combats evil.

The figure of Michael, then, is the result of a process of adaptation and resignification of ancient symbols and archetypes, which were reformulated to reflect the values and ideals of Christianity and other monotheistic religions. He thus becomes a synthesis of ancient warrior and protector gods, which are reinterpreted in the light of the Christian faith to represent a powerful angel, whose function is to defend the divine order and guarantee the safety of the faithful. This continuity and transformation of the archetype of the "just protector" highlights how the human psyche constantly seeks figures that ensure peace and spiritual protection, molding them according to the needs and beliefs of each era and culture.

Middle Ages and the Ethics of Chivalry

During the Middle Ages, the Archangel Michael became an essential symbol for the development of chivalric ethics, playing a central role in shaping the values and ideals of conduct of Christian knights. The figure of Michael as a celestial warrior and defender of divine justice resonated deeply with the ideal of chivalry that was emerging at that time, especially among the Knights Templar, who saw in him an example of spiritual strength, loyalty and courage. The cult of Michael directly influenced the formation of warrior morality, reinforcing the idea that war should be just and motivated by the defense of faith and divine order.

For the Knights Templar, Michael was an archetype of spiritual combat, symbolizing the eternal struggle between good and evil. These knights, who had dedicated their lives to protecting pilgrims and defending holy places, found in Michael a role model that transcended the physical valor of the warrior, embodying a spiritual and ethical dimension as well. They saw Michael as the leader of divine forces fighting against darkness, and interpreted his mission as an extension of this cosmic battle in an earthly context. During the Crusades, Michael was widely invoked as the protector of Christian armies, and his example inspired the knights to fight not only physical enemies but also evil influences that they believed threatened the Christian faith. The image of Michael as the defender of divine justice served as a reminder that the purpose of battle was not personal gain but the defense of faith and spiritual values.

Devotion to Michael was not limited to theoretical inspiration; it was embodied in the rituals and symbolic practices that were part of knightly life. Oaths and vows of protection were often sworn in his name, and many knights carried his image on amulets and relics as a source of protection in battle. These ritualistic acts reinforced Michael's role as the patron deity of warriors and fostered a sense of moral duty that transcended physical combat. The presence of his image served as a constant reminder of the knight's ethical responsibility to uphold justice and protect the vulnerable. He was venerated as a judge and protector, attributes that were reflected in the chivalric code of conduct, which called for virtues such as courage, loyalty, honesty, and compassion.

Michael's role in the Crusades cemented his image as a warrior angel and defender of Christian ideals. His figure represented a source of spiritual strength for Christian armies, and belief in his protection inspired warriors to see their battles as a continuation of the heavenly struggle between the forces of good and evil. Michael thus transcended his angelic role to become an active protector of Christian values in medieval society. The chivalric ethic, which valued commitment to justice and the defense of the innocent, found in Michael a model that combined combative strength with compassion and the protection of the most vulnerable. Michael's image was not just a symbol of strength; it promoted a view of justice as a moral duty that required both courage on the battlefield and rectitude in personal life.

Michael's association with the ethics of medieval chivalry helped shape the spirituality of the knights, who saw in him a guide not only for their actions but also for the development of a life of virtue. Michael was a moral guide who instilled in the knights the need to maintain their faith and integrity in the face of the trials of military life, promoting a way of life that harmonized religious devotion with the warrior ideal. His image as a defender of good and a spiritual protector reinforced the belief that the knights' mission went beyond battle: they were responsible for maintaining order and justice in society, a mission that reflected Michael's commitment to protecting good and fighting evil.

This transformative role of Michael as defender and protector was consolidated in the Middle Ages, profoundly influencing the chivalric ideal and the notion of a warrior morality committed to faith. For knights, Michael represented the meeting point between physical strength and spiritual purity, an ideal that encouraged not only heroism in battle, but also ethical responsibility and humility before God. He embodied a model of conduct that demanded sacrifice and righteousness, inspiring knights to fight for the protection of the vulnerable and to uphold a life of devotion and honor. Thus, Michael became a central figure in the spirituality of medieval knights, reflecting the ideals of a time when religion, justice, and military power were deeply intertwined.

Renaissance and Reformation

With the advent of the Renaissance, the Archangel Michael was reinterpreted in accordance with the new ideals of humanism, heroism, and moral perfection that characterized this era. Marked by a revival of interest in heroic figures and the exaltation of virtue, the Renaissance period saw in Michael an archetype of the just warrior and an embodiment of the lofty values of truth and justice. As a defender of cosmic balance, Michael became a symbol of the Renaissance ideal of harmony, where good is defended not only by physical strength but also by moral strength.

In the works of great Renaissance masters such as Raphael, Guido Reni, and Michelangelo, Michael is depicted with features of strength, beauty, and serenity that exemplify Renaissance aesthetics and the concept of idealized beauty. Raphael, in particular, immortalized Michael in postures of triumph over evil, highlighting his divine authority and heroic beauty. In Raphael's work, Michael appears with a serene countenance, stepping on the dragon in a gesture of complete victory over evil, a composition that reflects the humanist ideals of the period, where virtue and justice are presented as achievements of reason and moral purity. The focus on aesthetics and heroism was a way of exalting Michael not only as a celestial protector, but as an inspiring model for human conduct. This approach highlights Michael as an agent who protects cosmic harmony and inspires human beings to seek higher virtues, placing him on a pedestal of morality and courage.

With the arrival of the Protestant Reformation, the figure of Michael acquired new meanings, becoming a symbol of resistance and defense of the purity of faith at a time of intense religious and theological conflicts. The Reformation brought severe criticism to the Catholic Church, and Michael was reinterpreted as a figure of divine justice and spiritual integrity, representing the fight for truth in a scenario of religious divisions. For the reformers, Michael symbolized the fight against corruption that, according to them, had infiltrated the Church. He was associated with the idea of purity and fidelity to the true faith, and his image began to reflect the fight against evil not only in the spiritual sense, but also in the realm of ideological and doctrinal disputes.

In this new perspective, Michael was seen as the protector of Protestant communities, defender of the true biblical faith, and adversary of corrupt influences. Invoked as a spiritual guardian and divine judge, he assumed a watchful role, defending the faithful against distortions of the faith and protecting communities that sought a life closer to Christian ideals. For Protestants, Michael symbolized an unwavering fidelity to the sacred word, and his role as judge and combatant of evil became a metaphor for Protestant resistance to what they saw as the excesses and deviations of the Catholic institution. In this way, Michael embodied moral integrity and the fight for pure justice, values central to the reformers, who saw in him a spiritual force aligned with their own ideals of returning to purity and truth.

During the Renaissance and the Reformation, Miguel established himself as a figure who reflected the principles of heroism, justice and virtue. He was not only a protective and spiritual presence, but also a symbol that, through art and theology, inspired humanity to seek an ethical life aligned with higher values.

Miguel's image as a defender of good and an impartial judge was intensely reinforced, and he came to be seen not only as a fighter against the forces of evil, but as a source of inspiration for those who aspired to a life dedicated to faith and morality. .

This transformation of Michael's figure throughout the Renaissance and Reformation demonstrates his resilience and adaptability to the spiritual and cultural ideals of each era. He was shaped by the values of Renaissance humanism, becoming a model of perfection and virtue, and then reinterpreted by the Reformation as a symbol of doctrinal purity and spiritual endurance. These new roles reflect Michael's ability to resonate with human aspirations for justice, morality, and authentic faith, offering an archetype that transcends cultural and religious differences. Through his figure, the Renaissance and Reformation reinforced Michael's role as a spiritual and moral guide, encouraging the faithful to pursue a life dedicated to principles of integrity and righteousness.

CHAPTER 7. MODERN AND CONTEMPORARY RE-READINGS

Modern Spirituality and Esotericism

In modern spirituality, Archangel Michael has emerged as an inner guide and spiritual protector, playing a central role in New Age movements and esoteric practices. In a contemporary context where religious traditions often become fragmented or individualized, Michael is reinterpreted as a close and accessible presence, invoked to support personal development and the strengthening of emotional and spiritual integrity. He is not only a celestial warrior who protects against external forces, but also an archetypal protector against internal conflicts – helping devotees confront doubts, insecurities and fears.

In esoteric circles, Michael is often associated with the throat chakra, the energy center associated with communication, truth, and authentic expression. In this context, he is invoked as a support for those seeking to express their true voices and protect themselves from negative influences or "dense energies" that may hinder the fulfillment of their purpose. As guardian of the throat chakra,

Michael symbolically acts as an encourager of honesty with oneself and others, fostering clear communication and an authentic connection to one's values. This representation resonates strongly with the mission of protecting emotional and spiritual integrity, helping individuals defend themselves from external influences and sustain their inner truth.

In alternative healing practices and holistic therapies, such as Reiki and other energy healing methods, Michael is invoked to purify and balance the energies of those who call upon him. As a figure associated with protection and purification, he is seen as a force that clears negative energies and restores inner balance, offering a sense of safety and peace to practitioners. In this perspective, Michael transcends the role of a physical warrior to become a purifying presence and a source of emotional resilience. Many energy healers call upon him to assist in creating a "safe space" during their practices, where people can feel protected and at peace to release tensions and anxieties.

Self-help and spirituality literature also embraces Michael as an accessible guide and ally on the personal journey. Emphasizing his ability to inspire courage and authenticity, he is often suggested as a presence with whom anyone can connect directly, without the need for institutional mediation. This view of Michael reflects a contemporary spirituality that values individual autonomy and direct access to spiritual sources. In this way, he becomes not just a distant protector, but a close and personalized companion with whom each person can establish an individualized and intimate connection.

This new role for Michael as a spiritual mentor and advocate for self-knowledge reflects a significant evolution in his traditional role. In modern spirituality, he has transformed from a cosmic warrior and defender of faith to a figure supporting inner courage and authenticity. Michael is now invoked not only to protect against physical threats, but to guide people through their emotional and psychological struggles, fostering a life of integrity and resilience. He symbolizes the strength needed to face not only external battles, but also the internal conflicts that block personal growth.

Michael's resonance in modern spirituality represents an adaptation of his role to the needs and values of contemporary society, where psychological and emotional well-being are central to spiritual experience. By offering an image of security and support in times of uncertainty, Michael continues to inspire and guide individuals, providing a foundation for courage and personal authenticity. His figure thus transcends the boundaries of traditional practices and becomes an archetype for a spirituality that values self-knowledge, inner protection, and direct connection with the divine.

Popular Culture and Digital Media

In contemporary popular culture, the figure of Archangel Michael has taken on new forms and become a constant presence in films, series, literature and video games, being reinterpreted and adapted to align with the values and interests of modern audiences. This transformation reflects Michael's resilience as an archetypal icon that transcends the religious context and finds an echo in a society fascinated by heroes and narratives of conflict between good and evil.

In visual media, Michael is often portrayed as a ruthless warrior or as an angelic being of great wisdom and power, in line with the archetypes of heroes and protectors. In series and films such as *Constantine* and *Supernatural* , Michael is presented as a central or supporting character who acts in defense of humanity, confronting evil forces and protecting the world from dark influences. These portrayals reinforce his image as a defender of humanity and a tireless fighter against evil, evoking the Christian tradition of Michael as the leader of the heavenly armies and guardian of justice. When represented in action and fantasy stories, Michael takes on characteristics that combine angelic mysticism with the dynamism of the modern hero, becoming a character who is at once accessible and epic, suited to the taste for high-intensity heroic narratives.

In contemporary literature, especially in works of fantasy and supernatural fiction, Michael is explored as a multifaceted and often humanized character. In these stories, he is often presented as a being with moral dilemmas, torn between his heavenly duties and his ties to humanity. This portrayal adds depth to his character and allows the audience to understand Michael more closely and personally, seeing hlm not only as a distant angel, but as someone who faces internal conflicts, questions, and emotional challenges. The humanization of Michael in this literary genre adds new layers to his character and facilitates greater identification with readers, who see him as a protector who shares their personal struggles and existential questions. In many of these narratives, he is a reluctant protector or a character who ponders between duty and feeling, which allows for a more complex and emotionally dense portrayal than traditional representations.

Video games have also incorporated Miguel into their narratives, exploring him as a spiritual warrior in an interactive environment. In combat, action, and strategy games such as *Diablo* and *Bayonetta* , Miguel or characters inspired by him are portrayed as powerful heroes or legendary bosses that players can summon or face in epic battles. In these games, Miguel's image is used as a symbol of justice, strength, and resilience, allowing players to experience his figure in a dynamic and immersive way. The interactive experience of these games offers players the possibility of "living" the archetype of Miguel, directly confronting evil and assuming the role of a defender of good. This interaction with Miguel in the virtual environment reinforces his image as an icon of power and morality, translating spiritual and moral combat to the field of epic battle and allowing it to be experienced in a modern and accessible context.

In the digital and social media era, Michael has also become a popular symbol in online spiritual communities, where he is widely represented in visual content and disseminated in prayers, meditations, and motivational messages. On platforms such as Instagram, Facebook, and TikTok, he is evoked in inspirational images, associated with phrases of courage, protection, and resilience. These representations, often accompanied by iconic images of Michael as an angelic warrior, serve as daily reminders of protection and inner strength. In digital media, Michael's image transcends the concept of a religious figure to become a universal symbol of emotional and spiritual support, connecting people of different traditions and beliefs who look to Michael as a source of security and confidence in times of uncertainty.

Miguel's presence in contemporary popular culture and digital media reinforces his timeless appeal, demonstrating how he continues to capture the collective imagination and serve as a source of inspiration and protection. Adapted to different formats and audiences, Miguel remains relevant and timely, promoting values of courage, justice, and integrity that are universal and applicable to multiple contexts. His role in modern culture not only preserves his essence as a defender of good, but also expands his function to include characteristics that resonate with the internal and external struggles of contemporary audiences, showing that Miguel, as an archetype, is truly timeless and adaptable to the demands of each era.

Global Syncretism and the Figure of Michael

The image of Archangel Michael has transcended religious and cultural boundaries, adapting to various traditions around the world, especially in regions marked by religious syncretism. This phenomenon is evident in contexts such as Brazil, where Michael is revered in both Catholicism and Afro-Brazilian religions, such as Candomblé and Umbanda. In this scenario, he is syncretized with Ogum, a warrior and protective orisha who represents strength and justice, characteristics that resonate deeply with the figure of Michael. This syncretism not only expands the image of Michael, but also enriches his symbolic identity, allowing him to be seen not only as a Christian angel, but also as a warrior entity that reflects the qualities of protection, courage, and righteousness advocated by other spiritual traditions. In Afro-Brazilian religious practices, Ogum is a deity revered as a defender of the just and a symbol of strength, and this association with Michael highlights a cultural and spiritual bridge that allows the continuity and reinforcement of universal values of protection and the fight for good.

In Latin America, the figure of Michael takes on a popular character, being venerated in festivals that combine Catholicism with elements of local indigenous traditions. In countries such as Mexico, he is celebrated as a patron saint in festivals that include processions, dances, and rituals that blend Christianity with indigenous traditions. These celebrations have a cultural and spiritual depth, as they adapt the image of Michael to reflect the cultural specificities and needs of the communities for protection. He becomes a symbol of mutual protection between the divine and local spiritual forces, representing a link between heaven and earth. By incorporating elements of indigenous beliefs, the figure of Michael adapts to resonate with the spiritual and cultural experiences of the community, demonstrating the malleability of his image and its ability to respond to local aspirations. This phenomenon of cultural adaptation reinforces the idea that Michael is not only a heavenly guardian, but also a symbol of spiritual resilience that resonates with the needs of the people and reflects the desire for protection that is both close and universal.

In the East, especially in Christian communities in Asia, Michael is recognized and, in some cases, indirectly associated with protective figures from Buddhism and Hinduism. Although these connections are less explicit, Michael's qualities of combating evil and defending truth are paralleled by characteristics of local deities, such as Vajrapani in Buddhism, who represents the protective force against evil forces, or warrior deities in Hinduism who symbolize the defense of good. This association demonstrates how Michael, even in contexts less familiar to Christianity, can adapt and be respected as a protective spiritual presence. In Asian communities that interact with Christianity, he is often invoked as a defender of the faith and spiritual protector, showing that his attributes of combating evil and protecting the faithful resonate even in traditions that have different theological concepts.

Globalization and the expansion of Christianity have allowed the figure of Michael to be integrated into diverse cultures, creating a syncretic identity that reflects the human desire for protection and justice, regardless of cultural or religious barriers. This global syncretism highlights a universal search for values such as moral strength, courage and spiritual security, which Michael symbolizes and which resonate in different traditions and beliefs. His adaptability and the ease with which he connects with deities and protective spirits from other religions demonstrate that his image has been enriched over the centuries, becoming a figure that goes beyond the Christian faith to represent an ideal of divine protection and justice shared across cultures.

As he has been reinterpreted and adapted to align with local traditions, Michael has evolved from a warrior angel to a universal spiritual figure. He represents a point of convergence between different traditions, fostering a spiritual connection that transcends religious and cultural specificities. Ultimately, this evolution shows that Michael has become an icon of common values, such as the pursuit of justice, the protection of the innocent, and the fight against destructive forces. These values are innate to human beings, which explains why Michael continues to be such a powerful and relevant figure. In diverse contexts, his figure serves as a reminder of divine protection and as a symbol of hope and resilience, illustrating the power of syncretism to connect people through universal symbols and to strengthen the sense of community and spiritual protection across time and space.

CHAPTER 8. ETHNOGRAPHIC RECEPTION AND CONTEMPORARY PRACTICES

Testimonials from Devotees

Devotion to Archangel Michael manifests itself in a rich and multifaceted way, reflecting a deeply personal and emotional connection with his figure, which transcends religious traditions and adapts to the needs and spiritual perspectives of each devotee. In interviews and testimonies, many report that they invoke Michael in times of difficulty, seeking spiritual support in him to face crises, conflicts and personal challenges. In these accounts, Michael is described as a close and reliable spiritual ally, whose presence inspires strength, courage and resilience.

These personal narratives reveal that Michael is understood uniquely by each individual, functioning as a malleable symbol that adapts to different spiritual understandings and needs. For some, he is the quintessential angelic warrior, a relentless combatant against the forces of evil, evoking images of powerful protection and intervention in times of danger. For others, Michael is a presence of peace and security, a guardian who protects homes and families from negative influences and unwanted energies. This diversity of interpretations illustrates the flexibility of his image, which allows him to serve a wide spectrum of spiritual needs and desires, making him a figure capable of embracing multiple perspectives and symbolisms.

For many devotees, devotion to Miguel is not limited to moments of crisis, but manifests itself as a daily and constant practice. Miguel's presence is cultivated through simple rituals and practices, such as lighting a candle, saying a prayer or even keeping an image of him in a sacred space in the home. These symbolic acts are ways in which devotees make Miguel's presence in their lives tangible, establishing a spiritual bond that transcends formal ritual and becomes part of everyday life. Daily practice strengthens the sense of closeness to Miguel, who is seen not only as a protector in times of danger, but as a constant and reassuring presence, who accompanies and guides the devotee throughout life's small and big decisions.

Furthermore, devotees' testimonies highlight that the connection with Michael transcends conventional religious boundaries, illustrating the archangel's adaptability and universal appeal. Many report feeling a special connection to Michael, even without a formal or institutional religious affiliation. For these individuals, Michael represents an archetypal figure of protection and support, whose influence is not dependent on specific religious dogma, but is accessible to all who seek a spiritual force that inspires courage and confidence. This more individualized approach reflects a modern, personalized spirituality, in which the figure of Michael is perceived as a significant and accessible spiritual presence, capable of being invoked and felt in an intimate and authentic way.

Miguel's ability to transcend religious traditions and adapt to individual practices reflects his resilience as a spiritual symbol. In a contemporary context marked by plurality and diversity of beliefs, Miguel's image is reinterpreted in order to meet the specific spiritual needs of each person, transforming him into a guide that adjusts to the unique spiritual journey of each devotee. This flexibility is what allows Miguel to remain relevant and close, offering devotees a faith experience that is both universal and deeply personal.

In short, devotion to Michael demonstrates that he is seen as much more than a distant celestial being; he is an active and accessible spiritual presence in the daily lives of his devotees. This special bond between Michael and his devotees reflects a universal human need for protection, strength, and spiritual comfort, which Michael, with his welcoming and multifaceted figure, is able to fulfill in a unique way. This personal and emotional connection to Michael reaffirms his importance and resonance throughout the centuries, showing that he continues to offer an invaluable source of support and security to those who call upon him for guidance and protection.

Cultural Practices and Rituals

In many cultures around the world, Archangel Michael is celebrated in festivities and rituals that combine religious elements with folk traditions, reflecting the deep devotion and collective trust in his protection. In countries such as Mexico, Italy, and the Philippines, festivals honoring Saint Michael the Archangel occur primarily in September, the month associated with his day in the liturgical calendar (September 29). These celebrations include processions, masses, and traditional dances, representing both Michael's fight against evil and his role as protector of communities. These events are not only demonstrations of individual faith, but also expressions of cultural identity and unity, reinforcing Michael's role as a link between the sacred and collective life.

In Mexico, celebrations honoring Michael combine Christian elements with indigenous traditions, resulting in practices that represent a multifaceted devotion. Processions are adorned with symbols and vibrant colors, and traditional dances performed in his honor symbolize the eternal victory of good over evil, with reenactments of Michael defeating Satan. These festivals are more than just religious celebrations; they strengthen a sense of community and solidarity, bringing people together around a common symbol of protection and resilience. The figure of Michael, in this context, transcends the role of angel and becomes a cultural presence that connects spiritual beliefs with the history and traditions of the community, showing that his protection is seen as all-encompassing and present in all aspects of community life.

In Italy, Saint Michael the Archangel is also a powerful symbol, especially in regions where churches and shrines dedicated to him are central points of devotion. In places such as

Monte Gargano, home to one of the oldest shrines dedicated to Michael, festivals include pilgrimages and purification rituals, where devotees seek to renew their faith and ask for protection. These events highlight Michael's importance as a divine intercessor and defender of the faith, reflecting the belief in his ability to combat destructive forces and to ensure the spiritual and physical protection of his devotees. In Italian culture, he is not only a spiritual guardian, but also a symbol of hope and perseverance for communities that, over the centuries, have found in him the strength to face crises and challenges.

In the Philippines, the festival of San Miguel is celebrated with fervor, especially in cities and towns where he is considered the patron saint. Celebrations include parades, masses, and blessing ceremonies, where his image is adorned and venerated with respect and devotion. The festival, known for drawing large crowds, reinforces the faith of the population and highlights Miguel as an essential protective figure. Here, Miguel is seen not only as a spiritual warrior, but as a cultural and social defender who symbolizes the protection of the community in a broader sense. By participating in these rituals, Filipino devotees express gratitude and seek Miguel's support in maintaining peace and security.

In Afro-Brazilian practices such as Candomblé and Umbanda, Miguel is syncretized with Ogum, the orisha of war and protection, representing a fierce protector against destructive forces. In this context, Miguel/Ogum is invoked in rituals that include chants, dances, and offerings, through which participants connect with the energy of protection and courage. The association with Ogum allows Miguel to be seen as a defender not only of individuals but also of communities, strengthening his role as an all-encompassing protector. This practice of syncretism demonstrates Miguel's ability to move between different spiritual traditions, revealing a flexibility that allows his integration into diverse religious systems and strengthening his presence in the popular imagination. He is seen as someone who inspires courage and strength to face challenges, being a figure who transcends the limits of conventional religions to become a symbol of justice and resilience.

These cultural practices and rituals reveal that Michael is much more than a distant religious figure; he is a link between the sacred and the everyday, a protector who manifests himself in a way that is accessible and understandable to his devotees. By participating in these rituals, people renew not only their faith, but also their commitment to values such as courage, justice, and community unity. These events provide an experience of communion, where devotees reinforce their trust in Michael's protection and celebrate his fight for justice and good. Michael's universal character and adaptability demonstrate his resilience as a spiritual symbol, strengthening the connection between the divine and everyday life, and inspiring devotees to face life with renewed faith and courage.

The Figure of Miguel in Virtual Communities

With the advancement of digital media, the figure of Archangel Michael has found a new space to be celebrated and experienced in online communities and social networks, where his presence as a spiritual protector and symbol of strength is widely disseminated. In virtual spirituality groups, forums and pages dedicated to angelic figures, Michael is constantly invoked and discussed as a force of protection, emotional support and source of inspiration. These communities provide a welcoming environment for devotees to share their personal experiences, prayers and reports of miraculous interventions attributed to Michael's intercession, creating a network of spiritual exchange and collective support.

On social media platforms such as Instagram, Facebook, and YouTube, content related to Michael is shared in accessible, visual formats such as images, short videos, and guided meditations. These posts often include prayers and rituals aimed at protection, purification, and emotional strengthening, allowing devotees to interact with Michael in a practical and immediate way. On messaging apps such as WhatsApp, prayers, images, and messages about Michael circulate in family groups and among friends, establishing chains of faith that aim to invoke Michael's protective presence and strengthen the bonds of spiritual solidarity among participants. This virtual practice allows Michael to be present in the lives of devotees in a continuous and shared way, regardless of physical or geographical limitations.

Michael's digital representation adapts his figure to the modern context, promoting him as an accessible and immediate symbol that can be invoked in real time, allowing devotees to connect with him and with each other. This is particularly relevant for those living in dense urban areas or for people who, for whatever reason, have limited access to in-person devotional practices. Michael's presence on social media facilitates a collective spiritual experience in which he is seen as an ever-available protector, ready to be invoked in times of need and in practical ways, whether through a shared prayer or an instant message received. This digital approach to Michael's devotion creates a sense of community and togetherness that transcends physical presence, reinforcing faith and offering emotional support to devotees in different parts of the world.

These virtual communities expand the understanding of Michael, adapting it to meet the specific needs and challenges of contemporary life. In the digital age, he is often depicted as a protector not only against negative spiritual influences, but also as an emotional supporter of psychological and emotional issues such as anxiety, fear and stress, which are so common in modern life. In this sense, Michael becomes a symbol of psychological resilience and emotional protection, offering devotees a sense of comfort and security amidst the pressures of everyday life. This adaptation of Michael to the digital context reflects a more practical and personalized spirituality, where he is seen as a companion on the journey, close and accessible, who can be called upon at any time and for any type of challenge.

Miguel's digital presence allows for a dynamic and constant interaction with his figure, which helps maintain his relevance and significance in contemporary society. On social media, he is not only a guardian angel, but also a figure who adapts to modern aspirations and needs, resonating with those seeking spiritual support in a format compatible with the pace and challenges of today's life. This fusion of Miguel with digital media transforms him into a symbol of hope and security that is always within reach, fostering a spiritual connection that goes beyond traditional devotional practices and extends into the virtual world, where his image continues to evolve and adapt to new forms of spirituality.

Thus, Michael becomes a symbol that serves both traditional and digital spiritual contexts, reinforcing his role as a universal protector and spiritual guide. This digital transformation of his image represents an evolution of his role, showing that, even amid technological and cultural changes, the figure of Michael maintains his essence as a strong and protective presence. His image continues to be a beacon of protection, courage and emotional support, which adapts to new needs and remains alive in the imagination and daily lives of devotees, both in face-to-face practices and in the digital world.

CHAPTER 9. FINAL CONSIDERATIONS

The Universality of Michael

Archangel Michael emerges as a universal archetypal figure, transcending cultural and religious boundaries and occupying an enduring place in the spiritual imagination of humanity. His resilience over the centuries is remarkable and is directly linked to his ability to embody essential values such as protection, justice and courage – ideals deeply rooted in the human psyche. From his earliest mentions in sacred texts to his contemporary representations, Michael remains relevant, adapting to the needs and concerns of devotees of every era, culture and spiritual tradition.

Michael's universality is a reflection of his ability to resonate with a wide range of beliefs and practices, integrating both organized religions and esoteric movements and alternative spiritualities. He stands out as a defender of good and order, and is invoked in times of uncertainty and insecurity, offering his devotees a sense of spiritual security and encouraging them to seek integrity and justice. Michael's role extends beyond that of the traditional celestial warrior to become an accessible and approachable symbol of protection that can be understood in a variety of ways. In each context, Michael maintains his essence while allowing his devotees to interpret him according to their own spiritual needs, representing a flexible archetype that adapts to the changing world.

Michael's presence in a variety of cultural practices and rituals further demonstrates his adaptability and global relevance. In different cultures, he is often integrated into local religious traditions, such as Michael's syncretism with Ogum in Brazil, or his association with deities of protection and justice in other traditions. This fusion with local elements transforms Michael into a bridge between cultures, enabling the construction of a common ideal of fighting for justice and defending the vulnerable. Regardless of specific dogmas, he is seen as a universal protector who answers the call of all people seeking protection and spiritual security, reflecting the human search for a higher power to guide and inspire.

Michael stands out, therefore, as a timeless spiritual archetype, who not only survives historical and cultural changes, but flourishes in each new adaptation. He is a symbol of courage that stands the test of time, representing an ideal of moral integrity that transcends the limitations of any specific tradition. His unifying figure connects different religions, spiritualities and cultures, asserting himself as a significant and enduring presence that continues to shape and enrich the spiritual life of humanity. Archangel Michael thus remains a living force in the human imagination, offering a constant example of protection, resilience and the defense of good in an ever-changing world.

The Future of Devotion to Michael

Contemporary spiritual and social transformations have shaped and expanded Michael's role in the lives of devotees, reflecting an ongoing process of adaptation to the globalized and digitalized context. Globalization, cultural mobility, and the expansion of digital media have generated new forms of interaction with religious figures, allowing Michael to become an even more accessible and proximate presence. On social media and digital platforms, Michael is invoked and shared in real time, integrating himself into the languages and aesthetics of modernity. This flexibility ensures that he remains a relevant spiritual symbol connected to the challenges of today, allowing his role to adapt to cultural and spiritual changes.

As more people seek a spirituality that transcends traditional religious structures, Michael emerges as an independent spiritual figure, often accessed through personal practices such as meditations, self-help rituals, and protection practices. Modern spirituality, which emphasizes direct, personal experience, allows each devotee to interpret and experience Michael according to their own needs and beliefs. In this context, Michael becomes a personalized protector and guide, shaped by each practitioner's individual vision, which makes him especially appealing to a diverse and pluralistic audience. This movement reflects a central aspect of contemporary spirituality: the search for a spiritual experience that is meaningful and unique, where Michael is seen not only as a transcendent entity but as a practical and accessible force.

The advancement of digital media also offers new possibilities for devotion to Michael, facilitating the creation of global communities and support groups around his figure. In these digital spaces, people from different parts of the world can come together to share experiences, prayers, and devotional practices focused on protection and emotional resilience. In these communities, Michael is often reinterpreted as a symbol of personal resilience and emotional stability, reflecting contemporary demands for security and resilience in an increasingly unpredictable and complex world. Digital platforms allow his image to be shaped to offer psychological and emotional support, aligning with today's needs for inner balance and spiritual security.

The future of Michael devotion will likely continue to follow these social and cultural shifts, evolving to meet the new spiritual realities of a globalized world. Michael's figure, with his flexibility and adaptability, is uniquely suited to respond to these changes, and his popularity in modern digital and spiritual spaces suggests that he will continue to play a central role in the lives of devotees. In a context where cultural boundaries are less rigid and spirituality becomes more fluid and individualized, Michael has the potential to strengthen and inspire devotees in their personal struggles, while remaining a resilient spiritual protector who responds to the complexities of today's world.

Thus, Michael remains a living and dynamic force in contemporary spirituality, offering both an emotional and spiritual source of support for those seeking protection and resilience in the midst of uncertainties. His image continues to be reinterpreted and renewed, reflecting an ideal of courage, justice and stability that transcends time and adapts to the rapid pace of modern change. In a world where spirituality often distances itself from traditional institutions, Michael remains a symbol of moral strength and universal protection, demonstrating that his relevance and impact on people's lives will continue to grow, keeping pace with the needs and challenges of an ever-changing society.

Conclusions and Implications for Interdisciplinary Studies

Throughout this work, the study of the Archangel Michael has revealed not only the depth of his symbolism and influence, but also the wealth of possibilities he offers for interdisciplinary research. The figure of Michael transcends simple religious representation and emerges as a fertile field for exploring archetypal themes and the resilience of spiritual figures in the collective imagination, especially across different eras and cultures. Michael, as an adaptable sacred symbol, provides a framework for investigating how different societies reinterpret and integrate spiritual figures to meet their specific needs and adapt to the challenges of each era.

Michael's potential for interdisciplinary study spans a range of disciplines, including anthropology, psychology, theology, cultural studies, and digital communication. In psychology, Michael is an archetypal figure who can be explored in terms of his connections to the collective unconscious, representing the protective hero who symbolizes courage, justice, and protection from dark forces. Analyzing Michael's presence throughout the ages offers insight into the collective psyche of humanity and how societies express their spiritual aspirations and fears through enduring symbols. In theology and cultural studies, studying the evolution of Michael's image from antiquity to the digital age exposes the dynamism of religious imagery and illustrates the adaptability of sacred figures amid technological and cultural transformations.

Michael's potential as a research topic also extends to religious syncretism and the context of digital devotional practices. In Brazil, for example, the figure of Michael syncretized with Ogum exemplifies a rich intersection between Christianity and Afro-Brazilian religions, where Michael is understood simultaneously as a warrior angel and as a protector in Afro-Brazilian rituals. Investigating Michael's presence in non-Western cultures can shed light on how he is reinterpreted in diverse spiritual practices, enriching our understanding of his role in the globalized world and of the human capacity to find unity in symbols even in widely different cultural contexts.

Additionally, the study of virtual communities and digital devotional practices offers a new dimension for understanding the evolution of devotion to Michael in the modern era. Analyzing how Michael is invoked and shared on social networks and digital platforms can shed light on aspects of contemporary spirituality, where faith and symbolism manifest themselves and adapt to new communication technologies. Digital media, by allowing devotees to connect with Michael in real time and on a global scale, contributes to the transformation of religious traditions and creates new forms of interaction with spiritual figures. Thus, future research on Michael's presence in the digital environment can help reveal how spirituality is preserved and renewed in the modern setting, providing insights into the relevance of sacred figures in a society increasingly mediated by technology.

By synthesizing the complexity and universality of the figure of Michael, this work suggests that he will continue to be a relevant and inspiring topic for scholars interested in the impact of spiritual figures on the global collective imagination. Miguel is a living example of spiritual resilience, whose image goes beyond the barriers of time and resonates with different cultures and contexts. Miguel's ability to inspire, protect and connect devotees over the centuries reflects the strength of universal symbols and confirms the power of the collective imagination to sustain and renew fundamental values and aspirations for humanity. Thus, Miguel remains an invaluable source for exploring the dynamics between the sacred and the everyday, and his study can offer significant contributions to understanding the intersections between spirituality, culture, and technology in the contemporary world.

BIBLIOGRAPHY

- Aquinas, Thomas. *Summa Theologica*. Benziger Bros., 1947.
- Barker, Margaret. *Angels in Judaism and Christianity*. Bloomsbury Publishing, 2018.
- Berger, Helen A., and Douglas Ezzy. *Teenage Witches: Magical Youth and the Search for the Self*. Rutgers University Press, 2007.
- Boyce, Mary. *Zoroastrians: Their Religious Beliefs and Practices*. Routledge, 2001.
- Eliade, Mircea. *A History of Religious Ideas: Volume 1*. University of Chicago Press, 1978.
- Eliade, Mircea. *A History of Religious Ideas: Volume 2*. University of Chicago Press, 1982.
- Eliade, Mircea. *The Sacred and the Profane: The Nature of Religion*. Harcourt, 1957.
- Eliade, Mircea. *Rites and Symbols of Initiation: The Mysteries of Birth and Rebirth*. Harper & Row, 1958.
- Emison, Patricia. *Creating the "Divine" Artist: From Dante to Michelangelo*. Brill, 2004.

- Grimes, D. A., Benson, J., Singh, S., et al. (2006). "Unsafe Abortion: The Preventable Pandemic". *The Lancet*, 368(9550), 1908-1919.
- Hanegraaff, Wouter J. *New Age Religion and Western Culture: Esotericism in the Mirror of Secular Thought*. State University of New York Press, 1998.
- Haskins, Charles. *The Renaissance of the Twelfth Century*. Harvard University Press, 1955.
- Jung, Carl Gustav. *The Archetypes and the Collective Unconscious*. Princeton University Press, 1981.
- Keck, Leander E. *The Bible in the History of Christianity*. Fortress Press, 2005.
- Laurence, Jonathan. *The Emancipation of Europe's Muslims*. Princeton University Press, 2012.
- Mascetti, Manuela Dunn. *The Book of Angels: Turn to Your Angels for Guidance, Comfort, and Inspiration*. Macmillan, 1993.
- Melton, J. Gordon. *Religions of the World: A Comprehensive Encyclopedia of Beliefs and Practices*. ABC-CLIO, 2010.

- Mâle, Émile. *Religious Art in France, the Twelfth Century: A Study of the Origin of Medieval Iconography.* Princeton University Press, 1978.
- Orsi, Robert A. *Between Heaven and Earth: The Religious Worlds People Make and the Scholars Who Study Them.* Princeton University Press, 2005.
- Pelikan, Jaroslav. *The Christian Tradition: A History of the Development of Doctrine, Volume 1.* University of Chicago Press, 1971.
- Pinsky, Mark I. *The Gospel According to the World's Greatest Superhero.* Westminster John Knox Press, 2006.
- Possamai, Adam. *Religion and Popular Culture: A Hyper-Real Testament.* Peter Lang Publishing, 2005.
- Prat, Carole. *Esoteric Christianity and the Angelic Realm.* Quest Books, 2014.
- Sanders, Ed. *Judaism: A Very Short Introduction.* Oxford University Press, 2009.
- Sherry, Patrick. *Images of Redemption: Understanding Soteriology through Art and Literature.* T&T Clark, 2003.
- Snyder, James. *Northern Renaissance Art: Painting, Sculpture, the Graphic*

- *Arts from 1350 to 1575*. Harry N. Abrams, 1985.
- Steinauer, J., & Jackson, R. A. (2017). "Aiding Patients in Decision-Making about Abortion: The Role of Compassionate Counseling". *Journal of Women's Health*, 26(3), 215-221.
- Steinberg, J. R., & Finer, L. B. (2011). "Examining the Association of Abortion History and Current Mental Health: A Reanalysis of the National Comorbidity Survey Using a Common-Risk-Factors Model". *Social Science & Medicine*, 72(1), 72-82.
- van der Toorn, Karel. *Dictionary of Deities and Demons in the Bible*. Eerdmans Publishing, 1999.
- Vermaseren, M.J. *Mithras: The Secret God*. Chatto & Windus, 1963.
- Wilson, Stephen. *Saints and their Cults: Studies in Religious Sociology, Folklore and History*. Cambridge University Press, 1985.
- Wuthnow, Robert. *After Heaven: Spirituality in America Since the 1950s*. University of California Press, 1998.
- Zablocki, Sarah, and Liselotte Frisk. *Religion in the Age of Digitalization*. Routledge, 2020.

Milton Keynes UK
Ingram Content Group UK Ltd.
UKHW020050271124
451585UK00012B/1165